Picture History
of the
20th Century

THE 1930s

Richard Tames

FRANKLIN WATTS
LONDON • SYDNEY

This edition © 2004 Franklin Watts

Franklin Watts
96 Leonard Street
London
EC2A 4XD

Franklin Watts Australia
45-51 Huntley Street
Alexandria
NSW 2015

ISBN 0 7496 5667 0

First published in 1991

Design: K and Co
Editor: Hazel Poole
Picture Research: Sarah Ridley
Printed in Belgium

A CIP catalogue record for this book is available from
the British Library

CONTENTS

Introduction

The 1930s saw the betrayal of the hopes of the generation which had survived the First World War. The prosperity of the 1920s vanished with the collapse of world trade between 1929 and 1931. In almost every western country, democratic institutions found themselves facing challenges from both left – and right-wing extremes. For millions of ordinary people unemployment, which began as a personal disaster, evolved into a permanent way of life.

New technologies based on electricity brought some compensations in the form of cheap entertainment by means of radio and cinema, which enjoyed their hey-day. The socialist writer George Orwell remarked that it was a curious paradox of the free enterprise system that it condemned millions to enforced idleness and under-nourishment while enabling them to hear news, brought in seconds, from the other side of the world. For those who did have jobs, life was enriched by cheap food and housing and enhanced by the spread of electric power in the home and the advent of cheap motor transport. By the mid 1930s the worst, in economic terms, was over, but politically it was just beginning.

In 1936, Mussolini's forces were victorious in Abyssinia (Ethiopia) and Hitler's troops reoccupied the demilitarized Rhineland in direct violation of the 1919 Versailles Peace Treaty, yet unopposed by its democratic signatories. In the same year, a fascist-supported military revolt in Spain began a three year civil war which divided political attitudes throughout the West and provided a chilling preview of the greater disaster which was to engulf Europe as the decade closed. Meanwhile, in the Far East, Japan's full-scale invasion of China after 1937 marked the start of another conflict which soon involved the United States which had, until then, been preoccupied with its own problems.

Britain in the 1930s

To social critics of the time, Britain in the 1930s was not one nation but several. There was still the "Olde World" country, beloved of tourists with its sleepy cathedral towns and villages of thatched-roof cottages, and its farms where horses outnumbered tractors. There was also a new Britain, visibly growing on the fringes of London and the cities of the Midlands, where well-fed workers assembled cars and planes in shining factories built of glass and concrete and lived in neat, new suburban "semis".

But the decade was dominated by the problems of a third Britain, the Britain which had been created by the steam-driven industries of the Victorian era – coal, steel, shipbuilding and textiles. These were now in decline and the great, smoky cities of the industrial North, of lowland Scotland and south Wales were devastated as a result. Ironically, it was the threat of war and the need to re-arm that began to revive them as the decade drew to its close. Falling prices meant that most people in work were better off – but it certainly didn't feel like it.

△ The 300 mile "hunger march" of unemployed shipyard workers from Jarrow to London dramatised the plight of the depressed North. Here, Labour MP "Red Ellen" Wilkinson addresses a crowd in Hyde Park on their behalf.

◁ Fitting a child's gas-mask. Systematic air raid precautions began in Britain in 1935. There was a widespread fear that any future conflict could involve chemical warfare against civilians.

◁ Ramsay MacDonald, Britain's first Labour Prime Minister, also headed the coalition National Government 1931–35.

▽ Stanley Baldwin, three times Prime Minister, was a shrewd political manipulator presenting himself as a simple man.

◁ Edward VIII's abdication in 1936 in order to marry American divorcee Wallis Simpson divided the nation.

▽ After the "year of the three Kings", the coronation of George VI in 1937 marked a return to continuity.

Stalin's Russia

By 1929, Stalin had won the power struggle which had followed Lenin's death and driven his arch-rival Trotsky into exile. From 1928 onwards, he set Russia on a path of forced modernization through a series of "Five Year Plans" in order to create a "command economy".

Priority was given to heavy industrial projects and the collectivization of agriculture at the expense of living standards. These frantic efforts evoked much heroic idealism and even more brutal exploitation. Peasants who resisted the forcible take-over of their lands were liquidated either by mass murder or by deliberately caused famines.

To strengthen his hold on power even further, Stalin (Man of Steel) began a series of "purges" from 1935 onwards which led to the murder of thousands of loyal and bewildered Communist party members.

Purges of senior officers inflicted severe damage on the army with disastrous results during the Nazi invasion of 1941. Yet, throughout the 1930s, western admirers hailed the Soviet Union as a workers' paradise.

△ An Italian magazine of 1938 shows OGPU troops (secret police) about to bayonet an alleged Trotskyist sympathizer. Left-wingers dismissed this as Fascist counter-propaganda.

◁ The Moscow underground – a showpiece to dazzle foreign visitors who were carefully shielded from the harsh realities of state exploitation and terrorism.

◁ The tractor was a potent symbol of determination to overcome the traditional backwardness of Russian farming. But it was control of the land that mattered.

▽ Stalin developed a cult of personality which portrayed him as a universal genius – not merely a political leader but a poet and philosopher as well.

▽ A 1932 propaganda poster depicts members of the Communist youth movement – well-dressed, well-fed and cheerfully determined to defend the revolution. Art, like every other activity, was pressed into the service of political power.

Hitler's Germany

National Socialist (Nazi) party leader Adolf Hitler became Chancellor of Germany in January 1933. Within a month, the burning of the Reichstag (Parliament) had given him the excuse to extend his powers to rule by emergency decree. He began a process of "Gleichschaltung" (streamlining) which eliminated potential sources of opposition such as other political parties and free trade unions. A curtailment of civil liberties was, however, offset by a vigorous programme of public works and rearmament which bolstered national pride and dramatically reduced unemployment. Hitler believed that Germans were the descendants of an Aryan "master race" who deserved to rule the world. To him, Slavs and gypsies were useful only as slaves. Rabidly anti-semitic, Hitler initiated a programme to persecute German Jews. Determined to fulfill the Nazi dream of "Ein Reich, Ein Volk, Ein Führer" (One State, One People, One Leader), he annexed territories with German populations. Hitler then set about the forceful creation of a "New Order in Europe" by invading Poland in September 1939.

△ In May 1938, Hitler opened a factory to mass-produce Ferdinand Porsche's Volkswagen ("People's Car"). However, few cars ever found their way into the hands of German workers although many joined schemes to save for one.

◁ The destruction of the German Reichstag was blamed on a deranged Dutch communist, Marinus van der Lubbe. The new Nazi government moved very swiftly when it came to rounding up suspects and opponents.

◁ Nazi party members burn "un-German" books in May 1933. Hitler believed that he had a mission to purge Germany of any alien and, in particular, Jewish cultural influences.

△ Hitler reviews a march-past of Brownshirts, the Nazi militia, on a "Party Day" in the medieval city of Nuremberg, a favourite location for spectacular rallies.

◁ A shop in the port of Danzig/Gdansk sells Julius Streicher's racist newspaper and displays a poster saying "The Jews are our misfortune".

Spain's agony

In 1931, King Alfonso XIII abdicated and Spain was declared a republic. Despite regional unrest, the new republican government undertook many needed reforms. However, in 1933, a conservative government undid these reforms and crushed the workers' uprisings. In February 1936, a left-wing coalition was formed which consisted of Republicans, Socialists and Communists and became known as the Popular Front.

In July, General Francisco Franco air-lifted army units from Morocco to the Spanish mainland to challenge the government. In the Civil War that followed, Germany and Italy supported Franco with men and weapons, while Russia and Mexico aided the government, as did an "International Brigade" of idealistic volunteers.

Barcelona finally fell to the rebels in January 1939 and Madrid in March, after a siege of 28 months. The war cost perhaps as many as half a million lives, divided Europe like no other single issue and set the Spanish economy back a quarter of a century.

▽ Government troops, mostly without uniforms, cluster behind a makeshift barricade to fire on rebel troops besieged in the Alcazar (citadel) of Toledo in July 1936. Despite artillery bombardment, the rebels held out until they were relieved.

△ Francisco Bahamonde Franco was a career soldier and a firm believer in Spain's Catholic and aristocratic traditions. Personally austere in lifestyle, he ruled Spain from the time of his victory until his death in 1975.

◁ Dolores Ibarruri (La Pasionaria) was a brilliant public speaker who, during the Spanish Civil War, personified the defiant spirit of the republic and its slogan "No Pasaran!" ("They shall not pass!"). A life-long Communist, she then spent over 40 years in exile but later returned to Spain and politics.

▽ On April 26, 1937, German planes of the Condor Legion destroyed the ancient Basque city of Guernica in a matter of hours, killing some 3,000 civilians. Horrified Europeans saw it as a glimpse of what a second world war would bring. Exiled Spanish artist Pablo Picasso made it his masterpiece.

▽ A left-wing propaganda poster shows a death-bearing Nazi volunteer with the slogan "How the Church has sown religion in Spain".

The challenge of Fascism

Fascism originated in Italy in the 1920s and the Mussolini regime set the style for would-be imitators throughout Europe. Fascist movements had certain common features – rabid anti-communism, contempt for parliaments and civil liberties and a belief in the political virtues of violence. Fascist leaders tended to present themselves to the world as men of destiny who would lead devoted followers towards a glorious future.

By the 1930s, there were active Fascist groups in almost every European country. Left-wing opponents of Fascism, such as the British writer George Orwell, feared that it was acquiring the character of an international movement. Yet Fascism was in its nature intensely nationalistic and each group differed from each other in its aims and characteristics. The racist element which was so pronounced in Germany and much of Eastern Europe was seen to be largely lacking in Italy and Spain. Whatever its nature, however, Fascism made the most headway wherever democracy was unwilling to confront it.

△ Sir Oswald Mosley accepts the salutes of "Blackshirts", members of the British Union of Fascists at a Rally held at the Albert Hall.

◁ Dr Engelbert Dollfuss, Chancellor of Austria, proclaiming a new Fascist-style constitution in May 1934. Two months later he was assassinated by Nazis wanting union with Germany.

◁ Mussolini consciously used settings and symbols of Roman glory to stimulate support for re-creating an overseas empire in Africa and a militaristic state at home. He also secretly subsidised imitators like Degrelle and Mosley.

▷ Leon Degrelle, failed lawyer and leader of the Belgian Rexists. Fiery speeches, appealing to emotion rather than reason, were the trademark of Fascist leaders.

Turmoil in Asia

Throughout the 1930s the stability of Asia was threatened by struggles for independence and the emerging conflict between its two most important sovereign states.

China was divided between supporters of General Chiang Kai-Shek's Kuomintang government and those who favoured communism led by Mao Tse Tung. In 1931, Japanese troops seized the Chinese-owned state of Manchuria and in its place set up its own state of Manchukuo. This action brought about international condemnation and Japan consequently withdrew from the League of Nations.

In 1937, Japan launched a full-scale invasion of the rest of China which resulted in Communist and Nationalist forces finally joining together in an attempt to defy the Japanese troops.

Meanwhile, in India, Mahatma Gandhi tried to expel the British using non-violent and disciplined mass-action. The British responded with police crackdowns and constitutional reforms.

▽ In 1930, Mahatma "Great Soul" Gandhi organized a challenge to the government's salt monopoly.

△ Pu Yi, last survivor of China's last dynasty, was used by Japan as Emperor of their puppet state of Manchukuo.

◁ **General Chiang Kai-Shek, a professional soldier and head of the Chinese Nationalist (Kuomintang) government from 1928 onwards, he spent most of the decade fighting the Communists and trying to promote a neo-Confucian revival.**

▽ **Mao Tse Tung's 6,000 mile Long March (1934) took the communists to safety in remote Yenan, but less than one third of his 100,000 followers survived the ordeal. The Japanese invasion in 1937 (below left) forced Mao and Nationalist rival Chiang Kai-Shek into an uneasy alliance of resistance.**

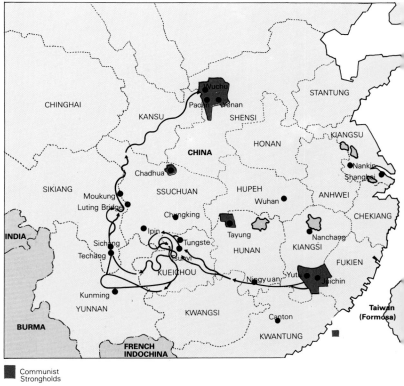

Communist Strongholds

The road to war

During the early 1930s, as a result of previous peace settlements, Germany was reduced to a shrunken, demilitarized state while Italy was a small, insignificant country. Both Hitler and Mussolini had grandiose dreams of restoring their nations to former glory. Determined to make Italy into a "Third Rome", Mussolini completed his conquest of Ethiopia in 1936. In 1939, he invaded Albania. To transform Germany into a "Third Reich", Hitler rearmed his nation and reclaimed the Rhineland in 1936. The two leaders also signed an alliance forming the Rome-Berlin Axis. By the end of 1938, Hitler had annexed Austria and dismembered Czechoslovakia by taking over the Sudetenland. After signing a non-aggression pact with Stalin in 1939, he invaded Poland.

The western European democracies, ill-prepared for war, reluctantly conceded that perhaps Germany had been ill-treated and Italy short-changed. As a result, the western leaders chose to appease the dictators by accepting their acquisitions and conquests. Only when Hitler posed a threat to Poland did they realize that their own security was endangered and prepared to use force.

△ Amiable Austria tempts a re-born Germany, symbolized by the hi-tech plane used by Austrian-born Adolf Hitler in his 1932 election campaign. The Anschluss (union with Germany) came in March 1938 and was over-whelmingly endorsed by the whole nation.

◁ German forces escort Polish prisoners during the invasion of September 1939. Despite gallant resistance, Polish forces were crushed in three weeks by the Blitzkrieg tactics of German mechanized warfare supported by superior air power.

◁ September 30, 1938 – British Prime Minister Neville Chamberlain returns from crisis talks in Munich to reassure cheering Londoners, "I believe it is peace for our time". The price was a German takeover of Czechoslovakia.

▽ The plane that became a legend, the Spitfire, tests its eight Browning machine guns which could fire 1,260 rounds a minute. Faster and more manoeuverable than the German ME 109, the "Spit" represented Britain's commitment to a strong air defence.

◁ German troops are welcomed as liberators by the German-speaking minority living in Czechoslovakia's Sudetenland border areas in October 1938.

Transport

Throughout the decade, increasing car ownership brought the convenience of private motoring to millions, but it was aviation that consistently captured the imagination as every year brought new headlines.

In 1930, Amy Johnson became the first woman to fly solo from England to Australia in 19½ days. In 1932, Amelia Earhart became the first woman to fly solo across the Atlantic in 15 hours 18 minutes.

1933 saw a world record for non-stop distance flying of 8,531 km, the first flight over Everest and the first around the world solo flight. In 1936, a world altitude record of 15,250 m (49,967 ft) was established. Regular airline services were also extended. Pan-American Airways inaugurated a trans-Pacific service in 1935 and a trans-Atlantic service in 1939. It was passenger liners, however, which still carried most people across the oceans and the launching of the luxurious liners *Queen Mary* and its French rival the *Normandie* showed that air travel was still seen by the masses as an adventure.

(Above right) Jim Mollison and his record-breaking wife, Amy Johnson.

▷ In May 1937, the German airship *Hindenburg* exploded trying to moor at Lakehurst, New Jersey, with the loss of 36 lives. In 1930, 48 people died when the British airship R101 crashed at Beauvais near Paris.

◁ By 1932, Imperial Airways had begun an airmail service to South Africa and introduced a passenger service to Singapore in 1933. In 1935, a flight from London to Australia, took $12\frac{1}{2}$ days – more than three times as fast as by sea.

▷ Sir Malcolm Campbell set the world land speed record of 500 kph (311 mph) in 1935 and the world water speed record of 288 kph (179 mph) in 1939. As a racing driver, he won over 400 trophies.

△ In July 1938, the British steam locomotive *Mallard* set a new world railway speed record of 203 kph. Most passengers got more benefit, however, from the electrificiation of some commuter routes into major cities.

▽ A 1930 Austin Seven (horsepower)–motoring at a price the middle classes could afford.

Science and technology

Throughout the 1930s, the United States maintained its position as a leader in both pure science and the application of technology to the improvement of everyday life.

In February 1930, astronomer Clyde Tombaugh discovered a new planet beyond Neptune, on the edge of the solar system. It was decided to call it Pluto.

In 1932, Karl Jansky of Bell Laboratories detected radio-wave emissions from stars, thus laying the foundations of a new science – radio astronomy.

The year 1930 saw Massachusetts grocers offer a new convenience food – frozen peas. Frozen meat and fish had been known for some years, but it had not been possible to treat vegetables in the same way until Clarence J. Birdseye discovered that "quick-freezing" preserved freshness without destroying texture and taste.

In the same year, Wallace Carrothers, a chemist at the Du Pont company in the United States, invented a new artificial fibre known as nylon. Its first use was for women's stockings.

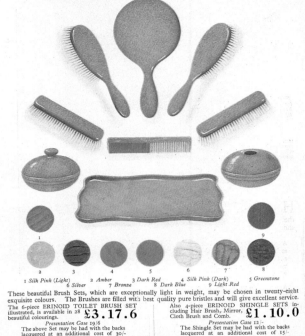

Erinoid Toilet Brush Set

1 Silk Pink (Light)   2 Amber   3 Dark Red   4 Silk Pink (Dark)   5 Greenstone
6 Silver   7 Bronze   8 Dark Blue   9 Light Red

These beautiful Brush Sets, which are exceptionally light in weight, may be chosen in twenty-eight exquisite colours.   The Brushes are filled with best quality pure bristles and will give excellent service.

The 6-piece ERINOID TOILET BRUSH SET illustrated, is available in 28 beautiful colourings. **£3.17.6**

Also 4-piece ERINOID SHINGLE SETS including Hair Brush, Mirror, Cloth Brush and Comb. **£1.10.0**

Presentation Case 19/6
The above Set may be had with the backs lacquered at an additional cost of 30/-

Presentation Case 12/-
The Shingle Set may be had with the backs lacquered at an additional cost of 15/-

Separate Pieces are also available in the full size set :—

Mirror 16/-   Hair Brush 20/-   Cloth Brush 12/9   Hat Brush 8/9   Comb 2/6   Tray 9/6   Shoe Lift 3/6
Powder Bowl, 4½ ins. 7/6   Hair Tidy, 4½ ins. 7/6   Button Hook 1/9   Glove Stretcher 5/6

HARRODS LTD   *Telephone* SLOane 1234   LONDON SW1

△ Harrod's – Britain's most exclusive store – offers plastic as the height of fashion and good taste. Its light weight was a special selling-point.

◁ New X-ray equipment at London's University College hospital doubles the number of patients who could be treated in a given time.

▷ The opening of Sydney Harbour Bridge in May 1932. It incorporated the world's longest steel arch and the widest carriageway – 8 lanes for vehicles, 2 tracks for trains plus cycle tracks and a footpath.

◁ A family watches an experimental television transmission in 1930 on equipment devised by the Scottish inventor John Logie Baird, who had produced the first television picture in 1925. The BBC began the world's first regular television service in 1936 but did not use a Baird System. The audience was limited to a few thousand near London.

▷ London's Battersea Power Station, designed by Sir Giles G. Scott and built between 1929 and 1935 was a potent symbol of the new importance of electricity in industry and in the home.

Radio

In the United States, listeners could tune in to a variety of radio stations. Long-running domestic drama series sponsored by detergent manufacturers gave the English language a new word – the "soap opera". In Britain, although it was possible to receive Radio Luxembourg and its advertisements from Europe, radio, or "wireless" as it was usually known, meant the BBC (British Broadcasting Corporation). Under its Director-General, John Reith, the BBC proclaimed to inform, educate and entertain. There was religious broadcasting every day and serious coverage of great national events.

In 1926, when the BBC had been established as a public corporation, some 2 million radio licences had been issued. This figure more than quadrupled by 1939 when 34 million people could hear a radio. Audience research revealed that the most popular programmes were variety, dance music and sport, that more women listened than men, more old than young and that peak listening times were at midday and in the early evening.

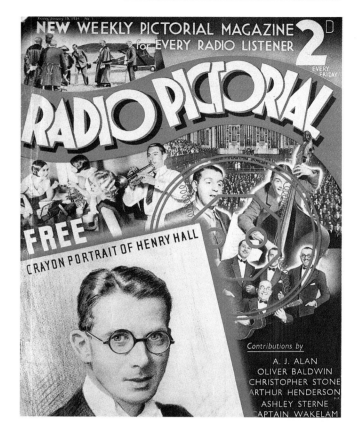

△ *Radio Pictorial* was one of a crop of specialist magazines aimed at the general listener as well as the technically-minded enthusiast. Notice the cover's emphasis on music. In 1990, Britain's biggest-selling magazine was still the *Radio Times*.

◁ The Radio Olympia exhibitions, begun in 1926, boosted sales of radio sets, as did live coverage of major public occasions like the 1937 coronation of George VI. Note the number of brandnames that are still in business 50 years later.

◁ A French advertisement for radios emphasises their technical features.

△ King Edward VIII broadcasts his abdication to the nation in 1936 via the radio.

△ Paul Robeson, the celebrated American baritone, poses in front of a typical 1930s radio. Music reached the largest audiences of anything broadcasting offered and listening became a family event.

▷ The young Orson Welles' radio version of H. G. Wells' science-fiction fantasy *War of the Worlds* in October 1938 threw New Yorkers into such a panic that many fled the city from supposed Martian invaders.

The Stars

Many films were made to cash in on the popular appeal of a particular actor or actress, so that the actual plot was a secondary consideration providing it made the most of the talents of the leading players. Ordinary movie-goers confirmed the producers' insight when they habitually referred to a new film not by its title but as "a Ronald Colman" or "an Errol Flynn" film. Stars were news on and off the screen. The most successful could afford to live lavishly but it was risky to live scandalously, or, like Bette Davis, to try to resist the power of the studios by picking and choosing the parts that they wanted to play. From the studio's point of view stars were a major investment, to be kept constantly at work unless they lost their appeal and then were to be ruthlessly discarded.

Some stars, like platinum blonde Jean Harlow, enjoyed brief but brilliant fame. Others, like Charles Laughton or Katharine Hepburn, laid the foundations of long careers and enduring reputations. But it was the producers who controlled the pursestrings.

△ Leslie Howard (1890–1943), born Leslie Stainer, specialized in the role of romantic and sensitive hero. He starred in *The Scarlet Pimpernel* (1934) and *Gone with the Wind* (1939).

◁ Shirley Temple in *Rebecca of Sunnybrook Farm* (1938). In *Bright Eyes* (1934) the foremost child star of the decade sang "The Good Ship Lollipop" and won an Academy Award.

◁ In *Mutiny on the Bounty* (1935), Charles Laughton played the tyrannous Captain Bligh while Clark Gable, "the King of Hollywood", was Fletcher Christian, the mutineers' tortured leader.

▽ Greta Garbo as "Queen Christina". Born Greta Louvisa Gustafsson in 1905, she dominated the 1930s in such films as *Anna Karenina* (1935) and *Ninotchka* (1939).

△ Marlene Dietrich, born Maria Magdalena von Losch, shot to fame in *The Blue Angel* (1930) and remained a screen legend.

The movies

In the 1930s, the "movies" became the "talkies". The addition of sound to pictures increased the importance of the script and the scriptwriter. Humour became less purely visual. The Marx Brothers, for example, combined traditional slapstick and stunts with a stream of wisecracks, double-talk and even musical gags. American slang, spoken on screen by gangsters, journalists or cowboys, spread throughout the English-speaking world.

Fashions and hairstyles were similarly influenced by the continually changing Hollywood modes. But if "the dream factory" offered glamour it also promoted morality.

From 1934 onwards, a detailed production code was strictly observed by the eight major studios which controlled 95 per cent of American film output. On the silver screen, love always ended in marriage and crime was never allowed to pay. However, the weekly newsreel ensured that everyone saw a little of what was really going on in the world around them.

△ Stan Laurel and Oliver Hardy – clowns of genius. Their efforts to be stylish or ambitious invariably ended in disaster and destruction much to the enjoyment of their audiences.

▽ *Gone with the Wind* (1939) was Hollywood spectacle at its very best – big stars, big scenes and a big, big budget. The result was a resounding success on both sides of the Atlantic.

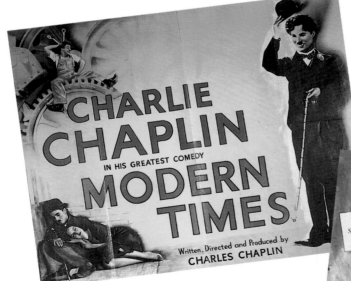

△ British born Charlie Chaplin, already a superstar by the 1930s, made a successful transition from silent to sound. *Modern Times* was his wry comment on the drawbacks of the machine age. Chaplin used a mixture of pathos and parody to represent the "little man's" view.

△ *The Wizard of Oz* (1939) starred a youthful Judy Garland as Dorothy, the heroine of a fantasy in Technicolour, a colour reproduction system perfected for feature films by 1935. Colour continued to be associated with some spectaculars or cartoons.

△ Sheet music for *42nd Street*, one of many dance spectaculars directed by Busby Berkeley. An ex-Army officer, he drilled mass-formations of chorus-girls to perfection and made inventive use of unusual camera angles.

◁ *King Kong* (1933) made sensational use of special effects. The terrifying "monster" gorilla was in fact an articulated doll which measured less than two feet high.

29

Music and dance

During the 1930s, a new style of popular music, called "Swing", attracted a widespread and devoted following. Big bands, capable of filling vast dance halls with sound, were the order of the day. Their bandleaders – Harry James, Benny Goodman and the Dorsey Brothers – were idolised, while many of the singers remained almost anonymous by comparison. Instrumental soloists were an important feature of the bands.

Black music began to develop in many ways. Actress Josephine Baker emerged as an international star. Mahalia Jackson, grandmother of modern gospel music, made her first recording, as did the legendary Billie Holiday and Ella Fitzgerald.

The folk music of the American West received serious attention from Woody Guthrie who gathered together many of his songs while living as a tramp. Hollywood countered with Gene Autry ("The Singing Cowboy"). Important inventions included the electric guitar and organ.

△ "Fred and Ginger", the inspiration for a thousand light-footed fantasies. Fred Astaire and Ginger Rogers were not only brilliant dancers but also highly competent players of light comedy in a string of film hits.

◁ "We're in the Money!" proclaim the chorus of Busby Berkeley's lavish *Golddiggers of 1933* – an ironic refrain for an America deep in depression.

▷ A 1932 dance marathon for engaged couples. Contestants danced around the clock until they dropped out from sheer exhaustion. Survivors could win cash prizes and brief publicity.

▽ *Porgy and Bess*, George Gershwin's "folk opera", set among the poor black community of a fishing village in the South, opened in New York in 1935.

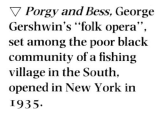

▷ "King of Swing" Benny Goodman (left) was the first bandleader to play jazz in Carnegie Hall.

Readers and writers

Compulsory mass-education in the late 19th century created a mass-market for cheap newspapers. A generation later, a paperback revolution and perhaps the enforced idleness of unemployment, showed that there could be a mass-readership for serious literature as well. In Britain, the publisher Victor Gollancz launched the "Left Book Club" to publish a new book each month on a topic of social or political concern. George Orwell's report on living conditions in the depressed north of England, *The Road to Wigan Pier*, was an early success. Within a short time the club had some 20,000 subscribers.

Contrary to expectations, cinema actually encouraged rather than diminished the reading habit as intrigued picture-goers ordered "the book of the film" from their local library. Even without the money from film rights, a best-selling author could become both wealthy and a celebrity. Edgar Wallace made a fortune out of detective thrillers, and lost most of it on high living, while Edgar Rice Burroughs made money out of a cinema tie-in with his *Tarzan* novels.

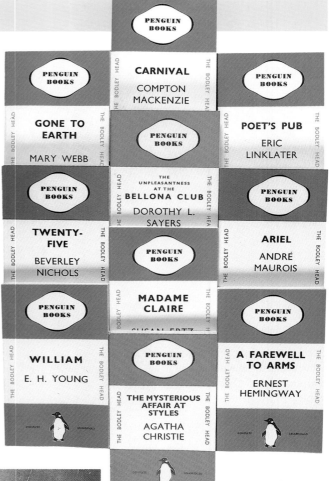

△ Penguin Books, launched in 1936, pioneered the "paperback revolution", publishing both "classics" and new works for less than the price of a visit to the local cinema. In due course they were to influence not only leisure reading but education as well.

◁ British novelist John Galsworthy, whose immense *Forsyte Saga* novel series criticised the moral emptiness of the propertied classes which made up the majority of his readers. He won the Nobel Prize for Literature in 1932.

◁ H. G. Wells' futuristic
Things to Come foretold of
world war and the
salvation of mankind. A. J.
Cronin's *The Citadel*
(centre) chronicled a
doctor's struggles against
social injustice. Walter
Greenwood's *Love on the
Dole* (below left) exposed
the human cost of mass-
unemployment. All three
novels were made into
successful films.

▽ P. G. Wodehouse
("Plum") won enduring
popularity as the author of
humourous stories
featuring young
Englishmen in wildly
improbably situations. The
most English of authors,
whose characters
inhabited a land of great
country houses and
eternal summers,
Wodehouse himself spent
most of his life abroad.

Fashion

In the the 1930s, a "smart appearance" was as much a matter of respectability as of fashion. Men were rarely seen outside the house without a jacket and hat. Even a working man would sport a muffler (scarf) and soft cloth cap. Women, likewise, wore hats and gloves on almost every occcasion and some people clearly distinguished between clothes for morning, afternoon and evening, as well as between town and country wear.

Fashion for women favoured tailored, close-fitting clothes to give a slim, elegant line. Although high street chain stores made inexpensive, mass-produced clothes more widely available for both sexes, it was quite usual for middle-class men and women to have clothes hand-made by a tailor or dressmaker. The sewing-machine and hand-knitting enabled the less well-off to cater for their own individual tastes as well. Tennis, golf and holiday cruises inspired a gradual trend towards more casual clothes.

△ **When the Prince of Wales wore a straw "boater", everybody wanted one.**

▷ **A Parisian tailor's catalogue offers the high society look.**

HIGH LIFE TAILOR

AUTOMNE-HIVER 1931

Extrait du catalogue de HIGH LIFE TAILOR, 112, rue de Richelieu et 12, rue Auber, Paris.

Pardessus droit, sur mesures.. **395 fr.**
Manteau, entièrement doublé
    lighting, garni fourrure.

HIGH LIFE TAILOR envoie gracieusement son catalogue de luxe de costumes sur mesures, sans essayage contenant la manière de prendre soi-même ses mesures strictement exactes, à toute demande adressée 112, rue de Richelieu ou 12, rue Auber, Paris. (Aucune succursale en province ni à l'étranger, même s'intitulant HIGH LIFE TAILOR.)

A toute demande de l'étranger un mandat de frs : 5 devra être joint.

34

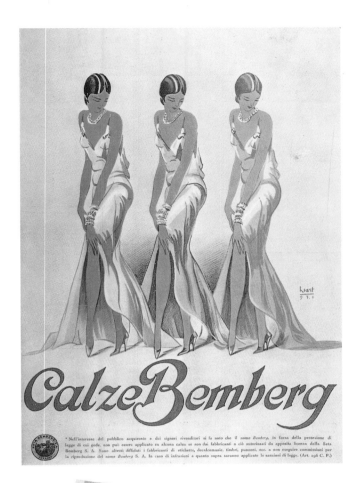

Calze Bemberg

◁ An Italian advertisement for stockings. Legs demanded adornment and the new artificial fibre, rayon, offered a cheaper alternative to costly silk.

(Below left) Extravagant night attire fashions were inspired by Hollywood's "femmes fatales". With central heating still a rarity, most people settled for cosier and more practical alternatives.

▽ Developing a sun tan was a new idea and suggested the luxury of Mediterranean holidays and winter cruises.

NIGHT WEAR GREAT JANUARY SALE

L.3. **Dressing Jacket and Nightgown** to match, made in Crepe de Chine trimmed ecru colour lace and tiny net frills. Nightdress sleeveless. Jacket kimono sleeves. Colours: Pink, Blue, Maize.

L.4. **Pyjamas** with bag, in natural colour Pongee with coloured spots. Neck and armholes trimmed silk to match colour of spots. Colours: Natural/Blue, Natural/Brown, Natural/

L.5. **Ladies' Pyjamas** in Surgo Twill Winceyette, coat shape with long sleeves. Collar, cuffs and pockets trimmed white. Trousers with elastic at waist. Colours: Peach,

Art and design

The 1930s' designers, adapting earlier trends to the new decade, sought to apply the principles of good design to objects of daily use. The emphasis was on "functionalism" (fitness for use) and an avoidance of unnecessary clutter or decoration for its own sake. Characteristics of this style could be seen as simple lines and economical use of space.

At the same time they also had to face the challenge of using new materials such as chrome, bakelite (an early form of plastic) or rayon, one of the first artificial fibres. They also had to design novel household appliances to fulfill the demand arising from the rapid spread of electricity into ordinary homes.

In Communist Russia and the Fascist states, designers and artists were often burdened with the need to show that their work portrayed and expressed approved political values. In Germany Hitler even organized an exhibition of "degenerate art" with which to underline the point.

△ In its stark simplicity, this steel chair sums up the design ideal of the 1930s, that of elegance and usefulness combined.

◁ The brightness and clean lines of the Hoover factory building in west London expressed the new face of smokeless industry based on electricity, another aspect of modernism.

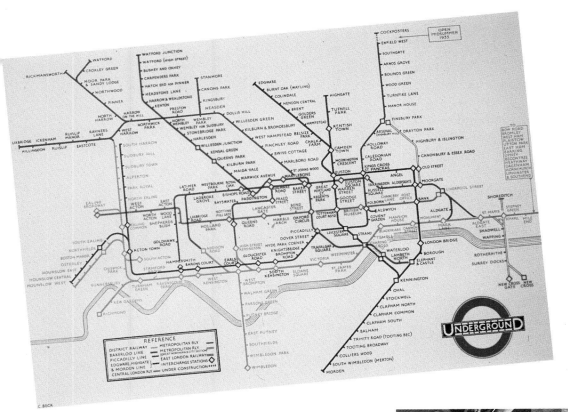

◁ A stylised map of the London Underground railway system – a design "classic" that was still in use, little changed, over 50 years later.

▽ The Seven Deadly Sins by German expressionist artist Otto Dix (1891–1969) showed the darker fears of a troubled decade. Following Hitler's orders, Dix was jailed in 1939.

▽ The Viceroy's house in New Delhi, designed by Sir Edwin Lutyens. The 1930s saw the completion of a project begun in 1912 to give India a truly imperial capital. "What a magnificent ruin it will make" observed the French statesman Clemenceau.

Sport

The development of radio broadcasting and cinema newsreels did much to further increase a mass-interest in sports. Thanks to these new forms of communication, fans no longer had to be physically present to be "spectators".

Cricket, which lent itself to radio commentary and detailed newspaper coverage enjoyed a golden age. It outshone football which was still regarded as being increasingly professionalised and which drew its support almost entirely from the ranks of the working-classes. Even star footballers earned little more than a skilled workman. The big money was in boxing, a sport which was seen as very brutal until a Board of Control began to regulate it after 1934.

For the long-term unemployed, sport and the gambling which was associated with horse-racing and the football "pools", became major ways of passing the time and a source of periodic excitement in an otherwise dull life.

Golf, tennis and motor racing were still seen as being almost entirely for the higher classes of society.

△ The 1936 Berlin Olympic Games were intended by Hitler to provide a convincing display of the racial superiority of "Aryan" athletes. This aim was decisively thwarted by a dazzling performance by American athlete Jesse Owens.

◁ American Jesse Owens set five world records in one afternoon in May 1935. At the 1936 Olympics, he won four gold medals for 100 metres, 200 metres, long jump and the 400 metre relay.

M.C.C. DEFENDS "BODY-LINE" BOWLING

"Legitimate—in Practice for Years"

Implication Against Our Bowlers "Improper and Incorrect"

BATSMEN'S HABIT BLAMED

County Clubs and Captains To Be Asked to Give Their Opinions

△ English bowler Harold Larwood's "bodyline" technique was considered to be an unsporting attempt to intimidate batsmen and led to bad feeling between England and Australia, and questions in Parliament.

△ Argentina equalize in the first ever World Cup final held at Montevideo in 1930. Home team Uruguay, however, went on to win 4-2. In 1934, Italy beat Czechoslovakia 2-1 and in 1938 defeated Hungary 4-2.

▷ American Helen Wills Moody, born in California in 1905, was known as "Little Miss Poker Face". She dominated the inter-war tennis scene, winning 19 major singles titles, including eight victories at Wimbledon.

Ideal homes

Low interest rates, the movement of people and the need to create jobs all helped to encourage large scale slum clearance and house-building programmes in many countries. New homes incorporated many significant improvements such as more hygienic and better equipped kitchens and bathrooms and, more importantly, electricity to provide light and power for a wide range of household appliances. But, in 1939, 90 per cent of British homes still relied on open fires as their main source of heating.

The United States was far more advanced in the use of major electrical appliances such as refrigerators and washing-machines. Few European families, however, could aspire to more than a vacuum cleaner although many did possess an electric iron. Even as late as 1939, a third of the homes in Britain still had no electricity.

Tastes in decor favoured bold, geometric designs, "streamlined" shapes and pastel colours such as pale green or pink. Characteristic design features of the decade include highly polished wood, moulded by steam into soft, curving lines complemented by shiny chromium and dark brown bakelite, a plastic used for small fittings.

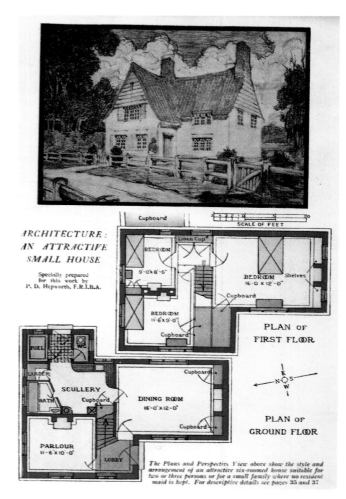

ARCHITECTURE: AN ATTRACTIVE SMALL HOUSE

Specially prepared for this work by P. D. Hepworth, F.R.I.B.A.

The Plans and Perspective View above show the style and arrangement of an attractive six-roomed house suitable for two or three persons or for a small family where no resident maid is kept. For descriptive details see pages 35 and 37

△ This model house still follows traditional cottage lines. It has no upstairs bathroom and incorporates such pre-electric features as a larder for food storage and an inside fuel store.

◁ This 1939 dream kitchen is centred on a solid fuel "Aga" stove, flanked by a broom cupboard (right) and a wall-mounted refrigerator. The floor and working surfaces are covered with rubber tiles and sheeting.

◁ This living room creates a bright and spacious feeling by avoiding clutter. Large numbers of ornaments, along with fussy patterns were thought "Victorian" and old-fashioned.

▽ A luxurious bathroom in Art Deco style echoes the legendary bath-houses of a Middle Eastern harem. But millions of people still had to be content with a tin bath in the kitchen, filled from kettles on a stove.

△ A page of electrical appliances from a store catalogue features side- and standard-lamps but also shows torches, an iron and a hairdryer. At 32/6, a hairdryer would cost more than twice as much as the weekly unemployment allowance for a single person.

Throughout the inter-war years, there was a marked trend towards smaller families. The reasons were complex – a shortage of marriageable men after World War I, unemployment, the spread of birth control, later marriage and the desire to have fewer children so that each could be better cared for and educated.

More and more children began to grow up in homes that were cleaner and less crowded, watched over by parents with more time to give them individual attention and affection. The trend was more clearly marked in middle-class than working-class homes.

Overcrowding at school was still the norm for those who could not afford private education. In 1932, official British rules set elementary class sizes at a maximum of 50 pupils. Seventy per cent of British children still left the educational system as soon as they legally could at the age of 14, but depression destined many for dead-end jobs.

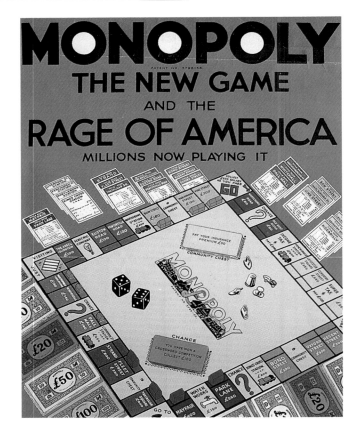

△ Board games became very popular as a cheap way of providing entertainment in the home for all the family.

◁ Friendly "nippies" provided speedy service at a Lyons' "Corner House" – the sort of place where young people could meet for tea or a snack before a visit to the cinema.

▷ In Britain, membership of the Boy Scouts reached a peak figure of 438,000 boys in 1938, with a further 161,000 in the Boys' Brigade. In Germany, the "Hitler Youth" was the only permitted organization for young people. It promoted physical toughness, comradeship, and a loyalty to Nazi ideals.

△ Comics were avidly read on both sides of the Atlantic, although the heroes and cartoon characters portrayed in them originated almost entirely from the United States. Comics also began to draw on the cinema for their stories.

▷ On the eve of war, Britain introduced a scheme of national registration for all citizens. This was needed for the administration of rationing, the "call-up" for the armed forces and in the interests of national security.

Personalities of the 1930s

Attlee, Clement (1883–1967), British junior minister in 1930-1 who refused to transfer to MacDonald's National Government. In 1935, he narrowly defeated Herbert Morrison to become leader of the Labour Party on the retirement of George Lansbury.

Beaverbrook, Lord (1879–1964), Canadian-born self-made millionaire who used his control of the *Daily Express* to crusade for "Empire Free Trade". At the time of Edward VIII's abdication, he arranged for the national press to keep silent over the sensational story.

Beecham, Sir Thomas (1879–1961), English conductor who used his inherited fortune to promote higher standards and a wider appreciation of classical music. A close friend and biographer of the composer Delius, he also founded the London Philharmonic Orchestra in 1932.

Bradman, Sir Donald (1908–), Australian cricketer who captained Australia (1936-48), achieved a Test match average of 99.94 runs and never lost a series.

Chamberlain, (Arthur) Neville (1869–1940), British Prime Minister who supported the policy of appeasement and negotiated the Munich Pact of 1938. He resigned his office in 1940 after the British defeat in Norway.

Chiang Kai-Shek (1887–1975), Chinese General who seized control of the Chinese Nationalist Party (Kuomintang) and put down successive army revolts to become effective dictator of China. From 1937, he co-operated with the Communists to oppose Japanese invasion.

Coward, Sir Noel (1899–1973), British actor/playwright whose plays include *Private Lives* (1930) and *Design for Living* (1932).

Dali, Salvador (1904–88), eccentric Spanish painter and designer who achieved international fame in the 1930s as a leader of the surrealist movement in the arts. Highly talented in a technical sense, he used his skill to create disturbing images from the world of dreams and subconscious imaginings.

Disney, Walt (1901–66), American film-maker whose cartoon creation Mickey Mouse became an international figure in the 1930s. Disney then moved on to full-length colour cartoon features such as *Snow White* (1937) and *Pinocchio* (1939).

Galsworthy, John (1867–1933), British novelist who sought to expose social changes and injustices. Creator of *The Forsyte Saga*, he was awarded the Nobel Prize for Literature in 1932.

Haile Selassie (1891–1975), crowned Emperor of Ethiopia in 1930, he tried to modernize his vast, impoverished country but was forced into exile (1936-41) by Italian invaders.

Harlow, Jean (1911–37), American film star whose sex appeal and gift for comedy brought her immense popularity before kidney failure brought untimely death.

Hitler, Adolf (1889–1945), megalomaniac dictator of Nazi Germany, called the *Führer* (leader). In the 1930s, he crushed all opposition to his rule and transformed Germany into a powerful war machine to support his aggressive foreign policy. After gaining territorial concessions from weaker nations, he invaded Poland, an act that started World War II.

Hutton, Sir Leonard (1916–90), English batsman whose 364 runs against Australia in 1938 set a Test record which stood for 20 years.

Louis, Joe (1914–81), the "Brown Bomber" who won the world heavyweight boxing title in 1937 and defended it 25 times to retire undefeated.

Moody, Helen Wills (1905–), American tennis superstar who, in 1938, won the Wimbledon women's singles title for a record eighth time.

Neville Chamberlain

Noel Coward

Oswald Mosley

Mosley, Sir Oswald (1896–1980), founder of the Fascist movement in Britain. He began his political life as a Conservative, then served as a Labour minister. His 1932 visit to Rome cast him under Mussolini's spell but, by 1934, his British Union of Fascists had swung towards Hitler and anti-Semitism. The Public Order Act of 1936, banning private armies and political uniforms, sent his movement into decline.

Mussolini, Benito (1883–1945), Fascist dictator of Italy, known as the *Duce* (leader). His imperialistic foreign policy resulted in the Italian conquest of Ethiopia in 1936 and the occupation of Albania in 1939. On the eve of World War II, he aligned his nation with Hitler's Germany, having formed the Rome-Berlin Axis in 1936.

Orwell, George (1903–50), emerged as a major writer with the publication of *Down and Out in Paris and London* (1933), based on his own experiences of destitution. *Burmese Days* (1935), a criticism of British imperial rule, *The Road to Wigan Pier* (1937), an exposé of industrial depression and *Homage to Catalonia* (1938) about the Spanish Civil War, were likewise based on first-hand knowledge. He also wrote satirical novels such as *A Clergyman's Daughter* (1935), *Keep the Aspidistra Flying* (1936) and *Coming Up for Air* (1939).

Owens, Jesse (1913–80), American athlete who won four gold medals at the 1936 Berlin Olympics.

Pu-Yi, Henry (1906–67), reigned briefly as the last Manchu Emperor of China (1908-12) before being appointed by the Japanese as Emperor K'ang Te of the puppet state of Manchukuo (1934-45).

Roosevelt, Franklin Delano (1882–1945), the only American President to be re-elected three times. His "New Deal" policies fought economic depression by creating employment through major public works such as dams and reafforestation projects, by payments to tide farmers over bad times and by new laws to support workers' rights. Through skilful use of radio, he used his "fireside chats" to bring himself closer to ordinary people than any previous President.

Simpson, Wallis Warfield (1896-1986), American-born wife of the Duke of Windsor, formerly King Edward VIII, who abdicated the British throne to marry her in 1937.

Smith, Bessie (1894–1937), American jazz singer and song-writer, known as the "Empress of the Blues", who recorded over 200 songs before being killed in a car crash.

Stalin, Josef (1879–1953), born Josef Vissarionovich Dzhugashvili. As general secretary of the Communist party in the 1930s, he used violence and terror to push through his policies of economic planning, industrialization, and collectivized agriculture in Russia. Opposed to Hitler, Stalin tried to form alliances with the European democracies. Rebuffed by the West, he signed a non-aggression pact with Nazi Germany in 1939.

Temple, Shirley (1928–), American child film superstar, who received a special Academy Award (Oscar) at the age of six. Her films include *Curly Top* (1935), *Heidi* (1937) and *Wee Willie Winkie* (1937). In adult life she entered politics and became a US ambassador.

Waugh, Evelyn (1903–66), British foreign correspondent and satirical novelist who converted to Catholicism in 1930, the year in which he published *Vile Bodies* and witnessed the coronation of Haile Selassie, an event which inspired his *Black Mischief* (1932).

Wells, H. G. (1866–1946), English science-fiction novelist who also combined scientific interest with social concern. *The Shape of Things to Come* (1933) prophesied the terrible effects of aerial bombing in future wars and was soon made into a film.

Benito Mussolini

Haile Selassie

Duchess of Windsor

1930

- Airship R101 crashes, killing 48 people.
- Amy Johnson flies solo from Britain to Australia.
- Uruguay defeats Argentina 4-2 to win first soccer world cup.
- Don Bradman sets first class cricket innings record of 452 not out.
- Coolidge Dam is dedicated.
- First sales of frozen food.
- Planet Pluto discovered.
- Invention of perspex and photoflash bulb.
- Gandhi leads civil disobedience campaign against British rule in India.
- France begins construction of Maginot Line frontier defences against Germany.
- Deaths of writers D. H. Lawrence, Robert Bridges and Sir Arthur Conan Doyle.

1931

- National Government comes to power in Britain.
- German airship Graf Zeppelin flies around the world.
- Traffic lights introduced in London.
- Empire State Building completed in New York as world's tallest building.
- US adopts "Star-Spangled Banner" as its national anthem.
- Captain Malcolm Campbell sets new world motor speed record at 246 mph.
- The George Washington Bridge linking New York and New Jersey opens.
- G. H. Stainforth wins Schneider Trophy with new air speed record of 408 mph.
- Walt Disney makes first colour film, *Flowers and Trees.*
- ICI produces petrol from coal.
- Deaths of ballerina Anna Pavlova,

opera singer Dame Nellie Melba, novelist Arnold Bennett and inventor Thomas Edison.

1932

- King George V makes first royal Christmas radio broadcast.
- Lindbergh kidnap case outrages America.
- Franklin D. Roosevelt wins the United States presidential election.
- Sydney Harbour Bridge opened.
- BBC begins regular television service.
- Vitamin D discovered.
- *Normandie*, world's largest liner, launched by France.
- Olympic Games held in Los Angeles.
- Salazar establishes fascist regime in Portugal.
- Sir Thomas Beecham establishes London Philharmonic Orchestra.
- The Soviet Union begins second Five Year Plan for economic modernization.
- Japanese puppet state of Manchukuo set up in Manchuria.
- Cologne-Bonn autobahn opened.
- Son of Charles Lindbergh kidnapped and found murdered.
- Deaths of thriller writer Edgar Wallace and brass band composer John Philip Sousa.

1933

- Hitler becomes Chancellor of Germany, followed by Reichstag fire and persecution of German Jews.
- Sir Malcolm Campbell sets new land speed record of 272 mph.
- Polythene invented.
- Franklin Delano Roosevelt inaugurates "New Deal" economic recovery policies in the United States.
- Prohibition of alcohol repealed in

America.
- British Film Institute and Odeon Cinema chain established in Britain.
- ICI produces synthetic detergent.
- Deaths of former US President Calvin Coolidge and British novelist John Galsworthy.

1934

- "Stavisky" riots in France against government corruption.
- Austrian Chancellor Dollfuss assassinated.
- King Alexander of Yugoslavia assassinated.
- German President von Hindenburg dies and Adolf Hitler declares himself "Der Führer"
- Luxury liner *Queen Mary* launched.
- Chinese Communist leader Mao Tse Tung begins 6,000 miles "Long March".
- The Soviet Union joins the League of Nations.
- London-Australia airmail service established.
- Driving tests introduced in Britain.
- Deaths of composers Sir Edward Elgar, Gustav Holst and Frederick Delius and of scientist Marie Curie.

1935

- King George V celebrates Silver Jubilee.
- Canada pioneers first broadcast quiz show.
- George Gershwin's folk opera *Porgy and Bess* opens in New York.
- Italy invades Abyssinia (Ethiopia).
- Persia changes its name to Iran.
- Pan-American Airways starts trans-Pacific service.
- American athlete Jesse Owens sets six world athletic records in one hour.
- Turkey requires all citizens to take a surname.

- Germany re-introduces compulsory military service.
- 30 mph urban traffic speed limit introduced in Britain.
- Lower Zambesi Railway Bridge, the longest in the world, opened to traffic.
- Death of war-hero and writer T. E. Lawrence ("Lawrence of Arabia").

1936

- Edward VIII becomes King and abdicates in favour of his brother, the Duke of York.
- Outbreak of civil war in Spain.
- Crystal Palace burnt down in Britain.
- Unopposed German troops reoccupy Rhineland in violation of 1919 Treaty of Versailles.
- Olympic Games staged in Berlin.
- Penguin Books established, popularising paperbacks.
- Hitler and Mussolini proclaim the Rome-Berlin axis.
- Mosley's Fascists' march through London's East End is thwarted by local resistance.
- John Maynard Keynes' "General Theory of Employment, Interest and Money" argues that governments can avoid economic depressions.
- Deaths of writers Rudyard Kipling, G. K. Chesterton and Maxim Gorky and of escapologist Harry Houdini.

1937

- German airship *Hindenburg* crashes killing 34 people.
- German Condor Legion bombers destroy Spanish town of Guernica.
- Marco Polo Bridge incident prompts Japanese invasion of China.
- F. D. Roosevelt signs Neutrality Act to keep America out of a European war.
- Billy Butlin opens Britain's first holiday camp.
- Insulin used to control diabetes.
- Jet engine and nylon stockings invented.
- Neville Chamberlain becomes British Prime Minister and the policy of appeasement begins.
- Irish Free State becomes known as Eire.
- Deaths of composers George Gershwin and Maurice Ravel, of inventor Guglielmo Marconi and of British ex-Prime Minister Ramsay MacDonald.

1938

- Launching of luxury liner *Queen Elizabeth*.
- Germany annexes Austria.
- Munich crisis ends in apparent resolution of the position of Sudeten Germans at the expense of Czechoslovak sovereignty.
- Schoolchildren in Britain issued with gasmasks.
- British locomotive *Mallard* sets new railway speed record of 126 mph.
- The ballpoint pen is invented.
- Vitamin E is identified.
- Nylon toothbrush introduced.
- First xerox photocopy made.
- Orson Welles causes a panic with his broadcast of H. G. Wells's *War of the Worlds*.
- Walt Disney releases first feature-length cartoon *Snow White and the Seven Dwarfs*.

1939

- Germany conquers Poland and divides its territory with the Soviet Union.
- Britain and France declare war on Germany.
- Russia invades Finland.
- DDT invented.
- Italy invades Albania.
- John Cobb reaches land speed record of 368.85 mph.
- Malcolm Campbell sets water speed record of 141.7 mph.
- Nuclear fission discovered.
- Deaths of poet W. B. Yeats, actor Douglas Fairbanks Senior, psychologist Sigmund Freud and Pope Pius XI.
- World Fair in New York.
- John Steinbeck's *The Grapes of Wrath* is published.

Index